# Night Shift

# Night Shift

Serena J. Fox

Turning Point

Published by Turning Point
P.O. Box 541106
Cincinnati, OH 45254-1106

Typeset in Bembo and Helvetica Neue

ISBN: 9781934999493
LCCN: 2009923986

Poetry Editor: Kevin Walzer
Business Editor: Lori Jareo

Visit us on the web at www.turningpointbooks.com

With quiet thankfulness, accept this offering—
family and friends,
who sustain and comfort me,
patients and caregivers,
who teach and guide me.

# Contents

# The City

# Night Shift

## I

*It is the end of the world, or just another night in New York City.*

Coffee from East Bay

Diner saves lives. Cup number two is stashed on the console. Paramedics radio in:
"We've got a thirty-six year old white male...forty-second floor...flat line... stretcher

won't fit...twenty minutes... fixed and dilated... request permission...

*Do you copy?...*

*Over and..."*


## II

In The Big Room, tonight,
hookers aren't yanking out their Narcan drips, so they can go back to work: "Hey, Baby,

how else do you support a $400 dollars a day habit?" Tonight, the toothless woman
about my age, covered with cigarette burns, and who stays with him, because he takes

care of her, is not having her stomach lavaged. No one is having an MI. There are no
messengers on backboards, cursing out City buses, no prisoners with split-open

heads, no baby-faced police officers, shot or stabbed. "Edward Brown?" There is charcoal
on the ceiling from the last shift. "Edward Brown!" A young woman motions, moderately

beaten around the face. "I'm Sheba. Jus' use Edward fo' de clerks." A nurse winks.
"What happened?" "Got beat up onna 'A' train." "Did you pass out?" "Almos."

"Do you hurt anywhere else?" No flinching around the ribs. She has beautiful breasts,
a sensuous torso. Her penis is propping up the gown. "I get beat up a lot." Her breasts are

better than mine. "Progesterone shots," she offers. Nurse gives me 'the eye'. I suture carefully.
It's a long gash in the middle of her face.


## III

There's a crowd in Room 13.
Boston Joe's tired of waiting, so he's telling a joke.

*Yes, I am my brother's keeper.*
It must have been an intern that took off his socks. An Aid runs to get a bucket, peroxide,

and Betadine. Boston Joe has 'toxic socks' and ulcers on his feet. I know it's Boston Joe, because I was shooting black-and-white photographs in Washington Square Park, last

Sunday, and it's the same joke. In the 8x10, his head is cocked, and a woman in jeans, behind a 135 mm lens,

*an other me,*
is reflected in his shades.


IV

*The end of the world is not a throne. It is*
*a triage desk. We file by. We are unloaded of a chief complaint, a brief, directed history,*

*social security number, and insurance card.*
**Al cheyt shechatanu/For the sin we have committed.**

*Of commission and omission. Of clarity and confusion. Of murmurings of the heart.*
*Insanity is an extraordinary and perfect state of mind—*

*glass to a caged bird, dangerous and clear.*
No one in the E.R.'s ever seen her,

The Inderal Lady; we talk her down on the phone. Her voice makes my palms sweat—
"i'm so afraid i'm having palpitations i'm sweating so badly i took some more inderal

can i take some more halcion can i take some more inderal how much halcion can i take
no don't call an ambulance i can't go out can i take another inderal can i take another

halcion if i tell you where i live they'll make me go out why can't i take another inderal
i'll take another halcion…"— All of New York City, plus half of New Jersey and

Long Island are camped out at the triage desk and I don't know where she is. "Take *one*
more Halcion, *no* Inderal." She'll call tomorrow.


V

But, what if she doesn't?

**Ut'shuvah ut'filah utz'dakah/and Repentance and Prayer and Deeds of Loving Kindness**
*avert the severe decree. Not repentance, but return*
Into the Big Room
with 'Baby Jane'. Her trach has plugged, again, and her son, in a red bow-tie, paces at the

door. We suction out the mucus plug. She's in a wheelchair, with a portable respirator, immaculate, no bed sores, dischargeable by morning. 'Locked-in', she cannot move or

speak. I think she may be 'in there'. Her son, who cares for her perfectly, is a lunatic. He wheels her to The Park, daily, all dressed up. He is wringing his hands in the corridor,

over and over and over… Speak to her gently, to the cavity behind her eyes. Should I praise her son, apologize for this outrage? Is she punished for some unavoidable,

parental sin, or rewarded for unforgivable, maternal caring. Does she pray for release? Curse me vacuously? Or,

## VI

thank G'd by the second for her obsessive, attentive, lunatic son?

*That is not to say that we can't*

*pray. Forgive to be forgiven*—**Unesaneh tokef**—*are we not on our knees?*

AIDS is an 'eyeball diagnosis'.

You know the second he walks in. Chief complaint: 'toxic prognosis'. You also know, Maureen, the nurse, will balk. "I'm not drawing blood on that one." She's in the back,

eating Chinese take-out. So, you've already drawn the lab tests and cultures, performed a physical, reviewed the C.T., sent the L.P. and ordered broad-spectrum antibiotics, an

antiviral, an antifungal. You wait for labs, because he's twenty-seven, and how do you tell him? The infectious disease specialist is on the phone. In less than two hours, you

use up any medical insurance your patient ever had—for life. You explain that we're waiting for lab tests. That we sent an HIV. That he might have AIDS. What we know,

for sure, is that he will wait four to ten days for a bed. It's nothing he hasn't guessed. Cherubic with fever and delirium, he swivels his head: "You a lesbian?" "Not that I

know of." "Can I give you a piece of advice?" He swivels two fingers in my face. "Use *two* condoms."

### Kol Nidreeeaay—All Vows.

*For the sin committed by compulsion, man to G'd, heart to sky, fist to breast-bone.*
*What is prayer, if not hope.*

*What is hope, if not compulsion.*

13

VII

Eem lo ahni li, mi li?
Eem lo achshav, matai?/If not I, than whom? If not now, when? *HOPE IS*

*an ex-nun in a red Mercedes. "We were only nuns, you gotta' forgive us." Hope is a red*
*nun in an ex-Mercedes. Only nuns, we gotta' forgive you. There are no bad habits in the*

*land of the exemplary. Eighteen years in Convent—first breath is a red ball of fire. Black*
*is blind. White is so white you gotta' be lyin'. Legs this pure are the gate-locks of heaven.*

*Children are sterile. Virgins are children. The ultimate Sacrifice for the ultimate Gift.*
*Angels are white, because they never went to the beach. Hope is a red Mercedes in*

*an ex-nun—flooring it fast. Nuns are us, only us.*

Muriel still dyes her hair red, although

VIII

she gets whopping hemorrhagic cystitis after chemo for bladder cancer. She has chest
pain from strictures. The strictures are from a ruptured esophagus. She knows this. She

just wants an EKG to be sure: "Muriel's in 6. She's asking for you. None of the other
docs will do an EKG." I think about skipping Muriel for once. I also want her company.

Muriel looks pasty. She's had bloody urine for a week. "My urologist gave me Valium,
but it's getting worse." We do the EKG. "I feel so ugly. Half my teeth are out. I can't

eat." "Heart's O.K. Can I get a blood count? Would you like a milkshake from East Bay?"
Hair, nails, make-up, suit are impeccable. The blood count is dangerously low.

"Can you come in for a few days?" "For transfusions?" I nod. She takes my hand. Her
smile stays with me. Teeth or no teeth, Muriel's my friend. Whoever's down there now

better be doing her EKG's.

IX

THE END OF THE WORLD IS
a Mizrachi model in a canary-feather mini skirt next to an article about 30,000 Muslim

women raped in Bosnia. The squeal of The Wheel.

Gilgul nefesh/Wheel of the Soul.

X

*World War III.*

When I leave the E.R., I go to *Dirty Harry* movies with D.B.,
my younger brother, the middle child, or maybe *Terminator* or *Rambo* sequels by myself.

Need deceleration. Too tired to write, shower, say my name. We grab a cab. The driver has
a massive beard and is driving backwards—"Hey, Doc, remember me? Been to Bellevue

twice this week. Asthma. Wanna admit me, but I got this cab and the novel. Next chapter's
about this guy—with asthma…" I also take dance classes like a maniac. But first,

I sleep. I sleep like a stone. I think death is like sleep, and sleep is #1,2,3,4,5, on my
list of priorities. Sleep to forget. Sleep to wake up not remembering. Sleep to be

reborn not knowing. Sleep to turn into the sun, because sun is so beautiful, and only
because it is so beautiful and infantile.

*Who are we? And what has become of*
*the world's Wisdom? A condom can save your life?*

Architects, artists, and hair stylists,
young ones, are dying, wall-to-wall, in the annex.

*Living in memory. Flesh of my flesh.*
After the pelvics and AIDS workups I've done tonight,

*you must be out-of-your-mind*
*to think I'd let anyone in.*

By the time I leave,

XI

another day breaks at the end of the world. All manner of souls file past the triage desk.
The line is up First Avenue, headed toward the Bronx. I feel inadequate. I count my

lucky stars. For the next twelve hours somebody else can check x-rays, prescribe
antibiotics, work-up fevers, suture lacerations, stabilize shock. Once, I deliver a baby

in the back of a taxicab. His mother has six other kids and shot up with the first
contraction. If I'm the only female doc, I've tried to see all women with vaginal

discharge. Privacy is not a commodity around here. What my patients really need—
and, by now, I'm stubbornly possessive—is food, shelter, education, and love.


**B'resheet/In the Beginning...**

XII

*CHOOSE LIFE—wind, spirit, laughter. Soul, being, light, breath...*
**Vay'h'ye/And it will be**

I will settle for a respite from violence.
*Inherit The City along with The Word?*

I'm so tired,
*living in memory, flesh of All flesh,*

that I cannot say my name, and I cannot say how one day follows another,
without dying first—
*and it will be,      vay'h'ye.*

# The Angio

My father lies at the end of my white coat,
witnessing his own angiography. He jokes,
winces occasionally. The techs are reading
*Malcolm X*. Two vein grafts are

occluded. The internal mammary artery graft
looks good in many different projections. In
this decade, we are redirected towards the
mammary, for our hearts' blood. It

strikes me that my father has no grandchildren.
A patient of mine had his coronaries done for the
third time with a graft from his gastric artery.
Truly, the way to a man's heart...

ha ha... We have bitten of the heart and the
heart is The Tree. The serpent recoils post-op.
Not one of us is ready for the next exposure.
I did not want to

bring him here, because I did not want him to
know how easily he fits into my pocket, and
to what lengths I'll go to keep him there. My
father observed the

autopsy of his father, who walked around Miami
for a week with a massive coronary occlusion,
and he can— my fingers at his temples,
holding all I ever need

to be— watch steadily as the
dye, serpentine, drips
down the screen.

## Heroes

Heroes give Kwell showers.
I take off the hat.
The note from the shelter says,
"...enlarged neck nodes..."
Her nodes are a natural disaster.
Posterior nodes drain the scalp;
the hat has to go.

Her scalp shifts like rush-hour.
The hat swarms.
I ask how long she's had it on;
she babbles at her hands.
I put the hat in plastic.

An orderly hums, gently, through his teeth,
shaves her without judging,
Kwells her head.
In the face of a great, sad, latex truth,
I am blank with awe:

Heroes do their jobs, gently.
Heroes have strong stomachs.
Heroes give Kwell showers.

## Grandbaby Doe

How you suffer me to die.
And oh my God how you
Suffer me to live!
Don't I know the flies know!
There one fusses on my lip,
My cracked, reptilian tongue,
Your 'dotted Q'.
Who dares censure eighty years?
Ties me to my bed?
You, who are too young and self absorbed
To even guess what fierceness
Keeps me fossilized, mid-air?
Will no one put a pillow to my head?
What freedom, liberty?
There is no place to shit
But on white sheets.
Some young whip has got to clean it up!
Almost has a smell.
Voices skin me, effortless,
Wipe and plan adventures after work.
Sign me out.
Same custodial mode.
What shift is this?
What season is it now?
I'll gum this nose tube out!
I'll pith you with an eye!
My butt is clean.
You're slithering out the door.
Blue dribble withers on my chin
And my blue manhood.

## The Train Wreck

Mrs. Kelly rolled her eyes and clamped her folded hands between her thighs. "I knew it was bad," she proposed, "when I stepped out the train—saw it severed—the head, I mean." She deferred to her teacup, where she could see the dead nun eyeing her, enviously, from the cream coffee.

"And you mean you've had a happy day, since? Surely, I don't know how," pronounced Siobahn, who was leaving Alexandria, Virginia for Saudi Arabia.

The face in the cup turned green. The nun's eyes floated like boiled turnips. "I couldn't find her body, anywhere. And to top it off," observed Mrs. Kelly, making a point, "an American medical student was running about taking pictures."

"I'm a good nurse," complained Siobahn, "but I'd like out of ICU. Why not sit in hospital with a sheik, rub him down, give aspirin, do blood pressure, make a bundle?"

"He is why I always hated Americans, until we moved here." Mrs. Kelly stared at the nun's head, warily, from the side, wondering if her sinuses were feeling poached, when survivors shirred her underfoot, until they noticed what she was.

"Would you like to see him now, Mrs. Kelly?" prodded Siobahn.

"I suppose I must," said Mrs. Kelly, gathering little force. Since they'd filleted Mr. Kelly's chest, right in his very bed, netting his struggling, greenish heart beneath a laparotomy cloth, Mrs. Kelly always saw the nun's head, floating in her husband's derailed chest, looking for a seat.

"I couldn't know," she whispered to her husband's ear, taking up his hand, like day old fish. "I'd never have pretended. She hardly even asked, just stared."

"Here he is," chirped nurse Siobahn, "lookin' a wee bit better. Makin' urine." Mrs. Kelly counted drops the color of her husband's skin. Siobahn recorded cc's in the chart, threw them down the sink, then suctioned down a tube. Mr. Kelly flopped.

His wife drew back. "I thought I'd be getting out—next crossing—home for tea." She aimed this at his chest. The nun's eyes bellied up. "There's blood about the edges." "That's nothing," said Siobahn and patted Mrs. Kelly's hands. "You're awfully jumpy. Come sit down. Drink coffee. I've got other patients to attend."

Mrs. Kelly smoothed her husband's forehead, chastised the nun, "Now you've got your seat—don't be followin' 'til I'm done." She almost took a sip, eyed her husband one more time, went looking for Siobahn.

## Belladonna

*Mad as a hatter, hot as a hare, red as a beet,*
*Dry as a bone*—pupils dilated as meteorites,
The stranger with the perfect pleats looked deep
Into your eyes, man to man, and slipped you some.

You went berserk, alone in your room, until José,
The super, swaggered back from bingo and called
The cops. *Bella Donna*—Beauties of Rome, tincture
Of Deadly Nightshade: one drop in the marketplace,

And pupils become the Discus, an iris-less magnet
To a Hero's hand. To *him*, she is worthy of wielding
In any game, an object more desirable. To *her*, he is
A mydriatic blur, overexposed beyond recognition.

For *him*, definition is not an issue. Skin anointed,
Stance youthful, eyes wide and black as a stabled
Beast. *Bella Donna!* She reinterprets: this doesn't
*Look* so bad. *He* is not so bad. What can happen, if

He takes me? It's broad daylight; my eyes will
Accommodate, before night catches up.

## I Want You In A Suit

There is no end to it
Pacifying anyone who
Demands a suck or cure.
Insurance pays for E.R. visits.

I can swim.
I can fix you while you wait.
The bottom of the tank.
Twenty rectals in a day.

CPR you out of the
Ocean of Heaven.
Puked, shat, peed, and
Spat on, I reel in

Twenty bodies in a day,
Organs plus-or-minus,
Appendages of all shapes,
Sizes, locations, prostheses.

I want *you* in a suit!

Socks, underwear, shirt,
Jacket, tie—the works.
I want to love you, slowly,
Through your pants.

I want your knees and my knees
To meet underwater. I want to suck
Cuff-links. I won't send you to
The lab. I don't want everyone

To know you. I am further than
You think. Not everyone is
Hooked on revelation, nor
Aspires to gels.

# Jackie's Night

A dim lamp orb
Night summer falling
Jackie hums to Tamar
At her breast
In the room that Richard built
Beyond the whirr of the fan
The round glow weights my lids
Steamrolled into the floor
I disengage
There is only Jackie
With a torque of light
On her neck
Breathing and
Rocking

# Northeast Coast Corridor

## I
Desire

is the fire out. It dwells in the last breath of live
coals, diminishing as we speak, that forms its
boundaries, defines its form.
It devours oxygen in a circle of widening
diameter, that keeps its own geometry to the end,
but, nevertheless, has more of death
and vulnerability to capricious air, at its


ash core, than the hunger that transcribes it.
As long as a few coals transgress, brightest,
most dangerous objects on
small mounds of combustibles, as long as they
are hunger driven, hope flares, fire takes issue.
It is no surprise that cities
burn themselves out from the inside out;


that their smoldering is contained; that they contain
all we wish to disinhabit. It is no surprise that
when the oxygen the coals
fight for is the oxygen outside the living edge
of the dying city, that is, belongs to someone
who desires to keep it, but does not
require it for hope, fire distempers its


refinements: ornaments on buildings, books, binders,
bread, what's born. The street becomes home.
It and its desires go last:
high-top sneaks, VCRs, CDs, coke, cash, kids.
Streets we stay away from are the living edge.

What we still can salvage of
suffocation, reduction, nothing left to lose,

desire without hope.


II

What We Sell

    is hope. What we purchase is desire.
The C-4 quad who smacks his lips and smacks, again,
        to order, ask, curse or crave is
    just another 'dude-brother', wrong place,
wrong time. "Jez' hangin'n 'ese dudes drived by 'n..."
        Even the African-American docs
    assume the new dude's Black, then


    vilify the rest of us for our assumptions,
ante-meridian so low, night and day so tightly
        locked in combat, day so utterly
    overcome by night, it doesn't matter what the color
is, it's just another shooting from Southeast, who
        beat the odds to end up in an institution
    without bars, as if they're necessary, as if


    the street hasn't wheels enough for all its swagger
gone to ash. The quad that comes to mind was so
        near release, his mother begged, and
    it was promised. But he lived. Rotobed, a cross and spit.
Living execution. He has a son. One more
        on the way. He's nineteen.
    There is no death by dying. Facial muscles


    master Morse code overnight. Lids blink—
*dot-dash dash-dot.* He lets them close. Lips pick it up—

*tztze, tz,tze.* A nurse who's good at
reading blinks and smacks talks slow and loud, as if the
wide-eyed just-another in the turning bed
were deaf and nearly blind, as well as
stalled, forever, in a twilight of


unmoving and unfeeling. Sensation from
the jawline up. Some thirst or hunger. Some flare in
eye that shows no fear, nor understanding,
just now, this moment, some truncate desire.
His mother brings his Nikes in. Stops thinking past
the day she's sifting through and
burns more brightly in her resignation. What


scrap of hope she carries finds an open window
to the chopper pad below, another cinder in the draft past
Medstar, Childrens', V.A., N.R.H.
(the National Rehab, where she's worked for
twenty years, a nurses' aide, so she should know),
skims 14th St., Mount Pleasant, then
Cleveland Park, Northwest, D. C. So


out of order. So in forever. We pay. He pays.
He's out. That is not to say we do not know him
inside out, his name, his -ostomies,
his smile, his Will, his breaking, when he wants
suctioning, when his lips are dry, what his son's
name will be. This alien room
is all we all never knew.

There are places in this city we won't go
that survive by race and recklessness
and nowhere else.

III


TRENTON


MAKES THE WORLD TAKES—*make-take,*
*make-take*... Under red, under neon. Under the arch
          two gray men fishing, same
     as under all gray girders in the world, the river gray, the
fish gray, the sunlight low and winter low and
          unprotected, showing tie and trestle
     for what they are, gray and steel and


          permanent, not interested in fish nor water
nor what they carry, nor what expectations
          welded them to one another.
     Do we shuttle past that truncate pyramid of stone,
before, or after, Trenton, where we pause,
          not a Metroliner stop—*make-take,*
     *make-take*...? A corner guardhouse?


          Prison, then. How often passed?
How many rivers? How many men or women we can't
          see for stone and gray and guarding?
     WORLD TAKES; we pace; they are impaled by
passage. Hourly. Of trains—*make-take,*
          *make-take, make-take, make-take*...


IV


Elizabeth Station


          stop oh my heart, where home lies, all the years,
all the days, yea, all the hours and minutes of
          this, my passing. There, old
     freight tracks, there, the spire, the imperious

courthouse, where once a grade-school girl with
      a full heart saw the knuckles of
   the fingers of two hands wrapped around


    skinny window bars, as if to place just some
amount of skin proximate to air, to breathing.
      There the stone arches, Main Street,
    a streak of red? The peanut vendor's truck (it would be
bags of chestnuts now), charred, sweet and acrid as the
      grown-away-from, ever-open.
    Arms. Our car. The rusted telephone she'd call from


    for a ride, if she were getting out today. EL-3-6411.
Same as it was, when she was four. Same as
    it is and still is, taken for granted, never
  and always, origin of anxiety only in
the going-away-from, for in the end, all life must bend.
     New York City—survival
    is irrevocable. But in what form and for


    how long? Home is an oasis in the burning.
Not a Metroliner stop—*make-take...make-take...*White stone
     columns (like the library across the street),
    bars (a prison window, then? ), a bad man
locked away, but so high up the tower, so close to sky,
     so divest of face and form,
    from where she would not turn away, it could


    be anyone—fingers, bars, dark and silhouette
against sky, white, Justice, stone? What if a woman?
    What would her children do?
    For to that girl, all women, who were not, had.
When would she get out, and what if the hands were small,
    or young? Not knowing who,
    or why, what if, or whether it was Just, or,

what precipitated getting caught, and knowing now
the things we come to know of just and chance and
      there-but-for- and what drives what,
on either side of bars, of Right and Wrong, that girl
was surer, then, that Just was fair and  Faith was just,
      and just the same, she would have
graced those fingers one more chance, for


who is safe, and, where are those children,
and why was no one looking up for pity, love, or hope?
      Home is and was oasis in the burning.
Why is it, every time she passes Elizabeth and
its courthouse—without getting out, without going Home—
      does she see those fingers, and feel,
so not-quite-safe, so compulsed-by, so bereft-of


expectation and the predictions that preceded them?
That is not to say we do not turn, and know and
      turn-away-from, fingers, bars, evidence,
burning. Trains pass through. This passes into.


V


Relativity


Industrial plain, a marshland, preens itself in glory.
Not a Metroliner stop. Reed cadets, legions, parade
      the spectrum yellow. Yellow,
not white, is the equalizer, late in the afternoon
continuum: Penn Station, Newark/Penn Station, New York.
      On the right— east, debris, incineration,
warehouses, railroad cars asphyxiated by swill, swill


radiant, petroleum prism, bending the slanting sun.
There, the fuming horizon, swaying on landfill,
      sulfurous, obscure, erect, sheer, shining—

City, Itself. West, left, an impossible angle,
sun within range of igniting the reeds, the weeds, the marsh.
Piling—black. In a wasteland—gold.
Perception: a marsh bird, covered in oil.


First, we sorrow. There suffers a white bird: polluted.
Then, reorient: why not black, bird, gleaming, manifest,
wings?


VI

Aesthetics

is the delicate eroticized. intimacy under glass.
testicles in a vise. impeccable line. infinite arousal.
City of cities, Thou shalt have no…
where to go but Up. high enough to promise; low
enough to see the sky scraped clean of ordinary
reinforcements. speed-walking with
the top in sight. beneficiaries of the


pooper scooper laws. so few parts per million
make it. obscenity is the phallus without the man,
as if the monument is what we're
after, as if the monument won't overtake the man.
"Tush Hospital," the house staff kibitz. "Tisch-NYU,"
an ER clerk capitulates, "hold please."
the Editor who comes to mind


whips out a business card and smirk.
"Send me something. Find out how rejection feels."
poetic Justice. shove a pious
finger up his pompous ass. no internal
bleeding. slow recognition: a decade, perhaps an art
or craft, ago–short story workshop.
undergrad. kicked out. he'd come

bombed. I'd gone home. (High Holy Days—
he doesn't know? oasis in the burning?) sole
      prerequisite: *don't miss class.*
transliteration—me: Class :: you: dog-doo.
still keep that card *and first line*, as in, "too bad,
      of all the first lines handed in
    yours was most…" immortality.


    percentage of net Worth. what passes through.
what this son's name will be. this room, this Will,
      this breaking. Tisch can name his pyramid.
    all livers look the same. late in the afternoon continuum.
at least the ER doors are open. not a window in the
      place. fluorescent. low and unprotected.
    not interested in what it carries, nor


    what expectations welded them to one another.
the Prisoner who comes to mind is massive,
      Monumental, black, a man.
    what eyes or claim? clerks recognize him from
the News. incarceration, why? he could be caged
      on Riker's, yet. complete exam,
    recorded for the Court. rectal underneath


    a sheet. vestigial dignity. anatomical evidence.
malingering, or not, and burning. cameras don't belong
      in ER's. penetration: key-turn-
prison-ward-in-Bellevue sound. there-but-for-the-
grace-of-. doors and bars I can turn away from to
      go back to work. no follow-up—
    for pity, love, or looking back—too slow


    to anger, to object. I need you, Park, tonight,
air to cobblestones in lungs and feels like snow and faith
      and *'If such…, then we know…'*

VII

Faith

    is the prison and the path. I need you, Park, tonight,
porcelained and dropping fast in vine-encrusted,
        darkness and degrees. Dog Run.
    The Met. dendritic trees. Dendur undisturbed at last.
benches rapt unto themselves. reservoir to reverie.
        gone small boats and bikes, barks, and
    unleashed yips and jumps. Dendur's dreaming's a


    soliloquy for Sunday afternoons in Spring,
suspension, pyramid to path, of plum upon
        air upon blossom upon air and blossom
and plum—prophesy, now, deeply inverted.
Central Park, South and West, sky and skyline, view
        to die for. low wall of stone.
    sirens out there perforating the whole of it. feels


    like snow. oblivion. merge, emerge, Emergency.
there are places I can go for warming. latte in a glass at
        Bruno's, watching Bleeker Street
    condense. Coles gym. Todaro's. Kiehl's on Third. Soho.
Jude's studio on Lafayette. Library of Performing Arts.
        Lincoln Center. ABT. NYCB.
    Jackie's loft, no—Jackie doesn't live here,


    anymore. but that was then and then is now.
just another quantum leap. pigeon stragglers, flying
        home, inflected in a flimsy skin of
    fragile, perspicuous ice, forsake the reservoir,
and there is no one here, and it is good, and, beware
        the dark, slow-dancing into might-have-
been-or-be, around the corner, one more

breath, before the buildings coalesce and
flesh moves under hand and fires fight for oxygen
the morning after. tragedy. we're
stable in a hypnogogic universe not even gods
would let themselves imagine—our -Ostomies,
our Ash, our hope, our wills,
our breaking. faith is desire-to-possess even


and beyond Will-to-survive, Above and
Beyond the object of desire. cruelty, alone, separates
Man from the ordered species, and
knowing and turning—back and away-from and
back again, clean—as if turning and cleaning are
one and the same, as if charring contains
Knowing. as if the object is contained. as if


the Object is desire. as if Monument
and Justice are men and the same, as if there is not
enough oxygen to go around.

## Another Drive-by

Drive-by birth—this mother snares a cab,
Shoots up, delivers, leaves her baggage
Backseat to the world—boy born, tab
Unpaid. The driver hasn't disengaged
The gears. Paramedics cut the cord.
The taxi twitches, swears, then disappears.
Sirens swaddle them and us in sordid
City night. Small body in arrears
For drugs, drugs lace a smile across a face
Devoid of motherhood, numb to need.
She nearly rolls onto him, takes his place.
We take her in to detox, warm, to feed
A son. Withdrawal fuels a newborn thirst.
Milky, dawn suckles day by dying first.

The Word

## Power not Peace

shit flows downhill he who loves
power gets to be king he who loves
love gets to be priest kings and
priests resurrect absolutes deny

existence of excrement and orifice
suffering is proof worship is suffering
he who suffers shit will not have power
he may have peace peace is indifference

to power and love Mr. Squillante at
peace stacks his meal tray with turds
smears his roommate with feces a man
wakes anointed screams and arrests

during the "code" Mr. Squillante dubs
feces on walls and himself Mr. Squillante
is neither king nor priest he does not
know what he is doing.

In Presumed Innocence Judge Iskar Asks,
"Why Belong to Physicians for Human Rights?"
during a Phone Interview to Cross-Examine
the Medical Affidavit for a Seeker of Asylum

All vows. America! America!
Cannot turn.    I lift my lamp.
She is an aftermath.

Her hand flew to her mouth.
Crepitant.    Consistent with.
*Forced too wide.*

She failed.    In the original.
To mention. *Rapes, her mother,*
Female circumcision.

Women sew their daughters shut.
Credibility loss.    *Sisters, blood.*
Commodity of virtue.

*Not seen since.* No external scars.
Labia minora,    clitoris excised.
*Alone, if she goes back.*

Facts as I have sworn them.
Never again.    Never stops.
Forsaken by.

But not by me. Yea though we
Walk. Valley of.    Shadow of.
Fear—No!

Judge Iskar, this is the least of what I can do.

## The Road to Çegrano, 1999
(with Patch Adams and Clowns, Skopje, Macedonia)

Pinpricks of poppies
Populations
Of them—

Supra-oxygenated
Arterial
Oblivious to

Camps and tents
Of no interest to
Scythes

Unregulated
Flaunting bright
Points in

Grass and fields—
The other side of
Fences.

In the camps
Children
With blackbird

Beak eyes
Scavenge trinkets
Touches

Kisses from
Strangers—
A busload of

Ferocious
Clown-doctor
Revolutionaries

Carrying
Medical
Supplies and

Angry
Armloads of
Peace.

One-on-one
With the villagers—
Six thousand here

Thirty-nine thousand
There—
Dust

Is the only
Accumulation—
Rust-colored

Covering the tents
And doctors
Without borders.

The clown-doctors
Come armed with
Red rubber

Noses
Electric-blue hair.
The kids riot for

Stickers
Attention.
They quiet for

Bubbles
Blown gently
Balloons for

The boy
Leg in a
Cast

Group photos
Promises to send
Pictures.

Thank G'd the
Fighting
Stopped.

What would they have
Done in winter
Summer?

But where to send
Them?
Back to the

Burning?
Over the fence
The fields?

Out toward the
Mountains—
Bubbles

Balloons
Boys, girls, bombs—
Poppies?

## Blood Holies

I

The Bridge

let us examine the compulsion of vampires
clinically: the blood return from the living to the
dying and dying that happens within chopper
range on the Beltway within critical time.

it comes up from blood bank barely thawed
in units sluiced from strangers who get orange juice
in exchange for life on-hold: it is no accident
that death and blood are utter aphrodisia.

it is thawing as we hang it: colder than
death—a cold the craving this conduit of accident is
becoming. we mortals have refined blood-getting to
the science we sanctify. it comes in bags.

we keep giving it and giving it. life is only
won in excess and she keeps waking up shaking her
head 'yes' and 'no' looking at us with eyes that
bleed of her humanness. this resuscitation is

state-of-art if not state-of-being and the
beneficiary is warm with blood pressure and
pulse and regains consciousness unit after
unit. the neck is unbearably erotic

as is death by rivers and the knife slash
amortizing throats of innocents over and over for
catharsis of life become addiction to dying and
the immortality in let blood. everything we

pump in pumps into her pelvis until many
blood volumes of many strangers thicken in the bed
the hemovacs and on the floor—a proteinaceous
monument to shared humanity and the

seduction of blood. humanity is a river
of bags of blood: a saturation of apocalyptic
proportion that monitors survival by excess
of arousal and genocide by unction with

undamned blood. there is enough blood
in rivers to salvage all mankind. but she will not
stop bleeding and we will not stop pumping.
Slovinia-Herzegovina slits its

throat. the Drina thickens as we pump
and—to spite all efforts—she exsanguinates.
!Na Drini cuprija! Bridge on the Drina!
it is the bridge not the river impales

the eye. "*They took people in their*
*vans and trucks to the bridges. They forced them*
*to lean forward. Sometimes they would shoot*
*them and sometimes they would*

*cut their throats. They threw them all*
*into the river.*" [Harden, Blaine. "Refugee 'Witnessed
Massacres Every Day' at the Bridges on the Drina".
*The Washington Post*. Friday, August 7, 1992.

p. A18]. Suljo Delic, 67, a retired maker of
blasting caps wears a black beret. he has lost his
journal. he says however [impossible to verify]
he remembers what he wrote: "*blood...*"

## II

Adzami-Oglan

Bosnia. November 1516. levy of the blood
tribute: Christian children collected without difficulty
from eastern villages. *...parents had hidden
their children in the forest, taught them*

*how to appear halfwitted, clothed them
in rags and let them get filthy, to avoid the aga's
choice.* They went so far as to cut off
one of their fingers with an axe.

[Andric, Ivo. *The Bridge on the Drina* translated
from the Serbo-Croat 1959. originally published as *!Na
Drini cuprija!* 1945. p.24.] !Na Drini cuprija! what
number of children is the right number of

children to circumcise the hills? a dark-
skinned boy ten years old arrives on the banks
of the Drina—one in the appointed convoy:
each horse with a basket each basket with

a boy. *Then the great terror. I shall lose
myself. It is against such fundamental menace that
perversion is invented...* [Stoller, Robert J. MD.
*Observing the Erotic Imagination.* 1985. p. 29].

this boy—carried away forever to a foreign
world to be circumcised become Turkish forget country
and faith and pass his days in service of the Empire
(*Note, how the perversion preserves*

*the trauma* [Stoller. p. 29])—this cold boy
waits overnight for surly Jamak the ferryman
who would not appear until the waters fell.
*Somewhere within himself he felt*

*a sharp stabbing pain which from*
*time to time seemed suddenly to cut his*
*chest in two [and] which was always*
*associated with the memory of*

*that place [where] misfortune was*
*open and evident [and] man, ashamed of his*
*powerlessness, was forced to recognize*
*more clearly his own misery...*

[Andric. p.25]. Visegrad—Slavic Muslim
city of 22,000 on the Drina overrun April 14, 1992:
*On that day, one of the Serb militiamen, a man*
*who was drinking plum brandy,*

*was asked by a reporter what was going*
*to happen to Muslim men in the town. The Serb*
*ran his finger across his throat. [Post. p. A18].*
*In the daydreams of perverse people...*

*what makes excitement out of boredom...*
*is the introducing of hostility into the fantasy"*
[Stoller. preface vii]. *The activity is perverse...*
*if the erotic excitement depends on...*

*the desire to hurt, harm, be cruel to,*
*degrade, humiliate someone, (including, at levels of*
*lesser awareness, the desire to hurt oneself)...*
[Stoller. p.7]. blood began dripping...

III

Fugue States

it is five years in the building chronicles
Andric: [Ivo Andric, born Travnik, Bosnia October 10,
1892. boyhood Visegrad, Sarajevo. university Zagreb, Vienna,
Krakow, Graz. house arrest WWI—three years

overlooking the Drina—member Young Bosnia
Movement and implicated in the assassination of Archduke
Franz-Ferdinand. 1919-1941 Diplomat Rome, Geneva,
Madrid, Bucharest, Trieste. career-end Minister

Berlin eve of WWII. death Belgrade March 1975.
the epic force of *The Bridge on the Drina* cited as justification for
the award—1961 Nobel Prize for Literature] bridge over the
Drina: about two hundred and fifty paces long

about ten paces wide save in the middle
where it widened into two equal terraces the *kapia*.
Christian children born on the left bank of the
Drina were taken across always to be

christened. all the others, those born on
the right bank and the Moslem children fished or
hunted doves under the arches of the *kapia*
as had their grandfathers and fathers.

white and delicate of clean cut Banja stone
stands the bridge with its eleven sweeping arches.
*Nothing could have been harder to imagine*
*than such a marvelous structure in this*

*desolate split landscape* [Andric, Ivo. from
'The Bridge on the Zepa' *in The Damned Yard and Other Stories*].
letter—the railway station at Slovonski Brod.
Max Levenfeld a doctor and a doctor's

son confesses: *I have thought this over*
*and over...still struggling against my decision*
*to leave Bosnia forever. Of course a man*
*obsessed with such thoughts cannot*

*sleep well* [Andric, from 'A Letter from 1920'].
The Great War over. Levenfeld served and survives
on all Austrian fronts: *Whosoever lies awake at*
*night in Sarajevo hears the voices of*

*the Sarajevo night. The clock on the*
*Catholic cathedral strikes the hour…More than*
*a minute passes and only then with a rather*
*weaker, but piercing sound does the*

*Orthodox church chime its own…*
*A moment after it…the tower clock on Bey's mosque…*
*strikes 11, the ghostly Turkish hour. The Jews*
*have no clock… so God alone knows*

*what time it is. Thus at night, division*
*keeps vigil… sometimes visible and open, sometimes*
*invisible and hidden…always similar to hatred,*
*and often completely identical with it.*

*Yes, Bosnia is a country of hatred…*
*hatred acting as an independent force…the instinct*
*of destruction or self-destruction and by strange*
*contrast… so much tenderness*

*and loving passion… unshakeable devotion…*
*such a thirst for justice… I wish you and our Bosnia*
*the best of luck in its independent life in a new*
*state…* 1576. Grand Vezir Mehmed

Pasha Sokolli—general and statesman of the
Ottoman realm: that cold boy. surely he does not
remember the Drina at Visegrad. *adzami-oglan.*
sixty years later—exactly—seeks only

to assuage his chest. life is only won in excess
and this resuscitation is state-of-art if not state-of-being:
by the Vezir's order and at the Vezir's expense the
building of the great bridge on the Drina begins.

IV

Arousal


a great mass of scaffolding then earthworks
arise carried out by forced labor. *Perversion may*
*be difficult to study in part because the gross*
*cases blind us to underlying subtleties.*


*If you are as I was, ...so struck by the absurdity*
*or monstrousness of the behavior that you stop thinking,*
*comfortable with 'perversion' in its accusatory sense...*
*[y]ou need no explanation. An example*


[Stoller p.10] *L., labourer, was arrested because*
*he had cut a large piece of skin from his left forearm*
*with a pair of scissors in a public park...He began*
*onanism at an early age, and read with*


*preference pious books. His character*
*showed traits of superstition, proneness to the*
*mystic, and showy acts of devotion. When*
*thirteen his lustful anomaly awoke*


*at the sight of a beautiful young girl who*
*had a fine white skin. The impulse to bite off a piece*
*of that skin and eat it became paramount...When*
*he had unsuccessfully pursued a girl he would*


*cut a piece of skin from his own arm...*
*Many extensive and deep wounds and numerous*
*scars were found on his body. During the act*
*of self-mutilation, and for a long time*


*afterwards, he suffered severe pains, but*
*they were over-compensated by the lustful feelings*
*which he experienced whilst eating the raw*
*flesh, especially if the latter dripped*

*with blood...During the whole crisis he*
*had erection and orgasm, and...felt greatly relieved.*
let us examine the physiology of arousal
clinically: blood-return from periphery to

pump. unit after unit—fright and fight.
definition: perversion is *the erotic form of hatred.*
it is no accident that death and blood are utter
aphrodisia. arousal is arousal:

everything we pump in pumps into her pelvis.
then the great terror: !Na Drini cuprija! this building
will eat us up Radisav the peasant whispers [p. 34].
even our children will be forced to

labor on the bridge. *Of course a man*
*obsessed with such thoughts cannot sleep well,* [Levenfeld
to Andric *Letter* 1920] and *[Levenfeld] would lie in front of an*
*open window in the room where[he] was born,*

*while the sound of the Miljacka [river]*
*alternated with the rustling of the leaves.*

V

The Feast of the Virgin

so a rumor spread: the *vila* of the waters
pulls down overnight what is built by day. Tools
disappear. masonry is damaged. the peasants
say that the *vila* who was destroying

the bridge would not stop until twin
children—Stoja and Ostoja—were walled into
the foundation. many swore they saw guards
in the villages searching for just such

a pair. (*guards were indeed going
around the villages...listening for rumors
and interrogating the people to try and
find out who were those unknown*

*persons who were destroying the bridge*)
[p.36]. in a village above Visegrad a stuttering
half-witted girl becomes pregnant Andric tells
us. women from the village bury the twins

stillborn after a difficult birth in a plum
orchard. three days later the mother begins to
look for her children. wanders down to ferry
and construction works. the men do not

understand. she unbuttons her coarse
peasant shift to uncover breasts painful and
swollen on which the nipples have begun to
crack and show blood and from which

milk flows with no resistance. no one knows
how to explain that her children have not been
walled up in the bridge. surely she continued
to stutter and live in misery. sought

always to assuage her chest. the tale
the children propagate is that guards found
twins—Stoja and Ostoja—took them from their
mother's breast by force. walled them into

the pier to stop the *vila* of the waters.
out of compassion a mason left narrow openings
in the pier so the unhappy mother could feed
her children. *Those are the finely carved*

*blind windows...in which the wild
doves now nest...[and from which] the mother's
milk has flowed...for hundreds of years...
the thin white stream, which at certain*

*times of year, flows from that faultless*
*masonry and leaves an indelible mark on the stone*
[*Drina* p.16]. there is a second legend the
children tell: of Radisav the powerful.

Serb no sword could harm. no chain
bind. Radisav the *rayah*—a Christian serf—sole
defier of the bridge. they took him by surprise.
drowned him sleeping. bound by silken

ropes—against silk the *vila* of the waters
could not protect him. there is a spot of hard
earth alone on the left bank and called for
a time Radisav's tomb where Serb

women believe: one night a year
in autumn between the greater and lesser feasts
of the Virgin a strong white light on that
barren spot falls direct from heaven.

VI

Sanctus

Andric writes: scaffolding in the darkness.
a small raft. on the planks a Christian peasant:
Radisav of Uniste himself. Sunday dawning.
workday as any other. news spreading.

capture, torture, execution. ...*The hodja*
*called out from the main mosque in the market-*
*place in a sharp clear voice... Radisav*
*bent his head still lower and the*

*gipsies came up and began to strip off*
*his cloak and his shirt. On his chest the wounds*
*from the chains stood out, red and swollen...*
*The gipsies approached...* first they bind

his hands behind his back. attach cords.
ankles stretching outwards and to the side.
legs wide apart. Merdjan the Gipsy places
the stake. two small wood chocks.

Stake pointed between the peasant's
legs. *Then he took from his belt a short broad
knife…to cut away the cloth of the trousers
and to widen the opening through which*

*the stake would enter his body…As soon as he
had finished, the gipsies leapt up, took the wooden
mallet and with slow measured blows began
to strike the lower blunt end of the stake…*

*The man was impaled on the stake as a
lamb on the spit…[T]wo gypsies began to lift him
up…So that the people saw him as a statue,
high up in the air,… high above the river…*

*Fear chilled their entrails and their legs
threatened to give way beneath them,
but they were still unable to move away or
take their eyes from the sight…* amid

that terrified crowd the inconsolable
mother kept up her search. only village children
high on the stone blocks of the *kapia* and up
in the bare trees answered [p.46-51]:

so, did the peasant of Uniste high above
the Drina become Radisav the martyr. among
the Serbs the women whispered: the *vila*
has buried the body of Radisav.

but in the night late swells a light
upon his grave—*thousands and thousands
of lighted candles* on that barren spot
direct from heaven.

VII

Apologia: In Silence is Safety

!Na Drini cuprija! humanity is the river
and the bridge. in time the Vezir began to conceal
a secret deep mistrust. *Every human action,*
*every word may bring evil... The Vezir...*

*crossed-out the first part of the seal with*
*his name. Only the motto remained: 'In silence*
*is safety.' He wiped that out as well. So,*
*the bridge was left nameless.*

Over there in Bosnia it shines in the sun
and glistens in the light of the moon [Zepa p.46].
apologia: Whosoever lies awake! if you be
as I be: so transfixed by the monstrous

and the monumental—such a thirst
for justice become addiction to arousal the
mortal and immortal in let blood—then your
mind cannot stop whispering:

night in a trauma unit. a newspaper
report at a moment of great fatigue. proteinaceous
shared humanity. a Nobel laureate's mastery
of its telling—all humankind's

soft sad self-destruction: blood started
dripping from the bridges shortly after May 10.
*We found a piece of brain, some skull with*
*hair on it and some children's shoes.*

*They made us throw it all into the Drina.*
*On one of the bodies four fingers on the left hand*
*were freshly cut off.* note how the perversion
preserves the trauma:

in silence—safety. surely a human being
obsessed with such thoughts cannot sleep well.
Delic has lost his journal and all record
of the atrocities. he says however

[impossible to verify]: he remembers
what he wrote.

SELECTED BIBLIOGRAPHY

"Refugee 'Witnessed Massacres Every Day' at the Bridges on the Drina" by Blaine Harden.
*The Washington Post*. Friday, August 7, 1992. p. A18.

Andric, Ivo. *The Bridge on the Drina*. translated from the Serbo-Croat by Lovett F. Edwards.
The University of Chicago Press. Chicago. 1977. MacMillan Publishing Company, Inc.

Andric, Ivo. 'The Bridge on the Zepa' and 'Letter from 1920' in *The Damned Yard and
Other Stories*. edited by Celia Hawkesworth. Forest Books, London and Boston. Dereta,
Belgrade 1992.

Stoller, Robert J., M.D. *The Observing of the Erotic Imagination*. Yale University Press.
New Haven and London. 1985.

# After the Reading

community of pines. meeting-house of
mountains. studded podium of sky. clasped
in the valley of the consummate
telling, Prayer, alone, can back-light
revelation. mist of the martyrs. honey of
the herd. Shabbos Candles, we have words
for you, who stutter and then gleam
a small white glory.

# The Breath

# 551,880,000 Breaths

The yogi measures his span of life not by numbers of days, but of breaths. Since breathing is lengthened in Pranayama, its practice leads to longevity... The normal rate of breathing is 21,600 breaths inhaled and exhaled every twenty-four hours.
—BKS Iyengar *Light on Yoga*

I

551,880,000 breaths per
Lifetime. Hmm—
What can one say?
Except that the living
Count backwards.

II

Lungers count in ones.
25% of body energy
Exhausted for each flat
Heave of the diaphragm.
When the wheezing starts,
They sleep upright
With nasal prongs, one eye
On the mirror.

III

What about respirators?
I can paralyze you with an
Index finger, as effortlessly
As I brush your eyelashes,
Making sure you're down.
I set breaths per minute, by
Pressing digits in a square.

Another plunge of my finger
Slides you beyond consciousness
And memory. I hope sedation
Lets you dream, gloriously and
Elusively, beyond pain, so we can
Turn you, change the dressing
Where your sternum is no longer
Intact. A few millimeters—

All that separates us,
Phalanx from pectoral flap,
You from me.
A thickness worth pause,
More so, if my finger can
Change outcome with the
Number of your breath.

IV

I am counting backwards for her. She is
Twenty-one. Her first child, delivered by
C-section, is fine, her hemorrhaging stopped,
Blood pressure controlled. But, in her brain,
The ventricles overflow with blood, and the
Gray matter swells like wet cement.

A young woman dies in my arms three times:

Minutes from now, when her heart stops and
The bell empties, dislocated, like the click of
The ventilator 'off' switch, that dangles with
The IV tubing, dispensing zeroes in micro-drops;

Six-thirty p.m. this October evening, under my
Hand, when she fit criteria for clinical brain
Death, and my hand waited so long on the
Pendulum of her left ribs, I couldn't tell who
Was not breathing, she or I; and

Yesterday, when her brainstem flooded, and
She offered her last breath, but no one noticed,
Because the machine metronomed a hymn of
Pious ins and outs, unrelenting as a monk.

I am counting backwards for her, because,
When the ringing stops, she will not unburden
Her last breath, so how can her heart know
When to fly?

V

April is running on the beach.
She is long-legged. There is
Nothing mincing about her.
She does a headstand in her bikini.
Woodstock, the golden lab pup,
Falls into me, licking my foot.

Early, early this morning, running, I left
Footprints in the tractored sand: pigeon-toed
Duck-footed, backwards, singing whatever
Came to mind, singing with my mother's
Voice in my ear. *Green grow the lilacs all*
*Covered with dew. /I'm lonely my darling*
*Since parting with you...* The long-legged
Ocean is in my ear. I am standing on my bed
To reach my mother's shoulder as she rocks,
Back and forth, back and forth, with my
Sandbag head, singing a song I'll sing to my
Children. I know all the songs she'll sing to her

Grandchildren; how her clavicle accommodates a
Cheekbone; how, to one eye half-closed, her lips
Loom; how an incisor indents that lip; how an earlobe
Rosettes, garnet-pinched. I want my children (if
I ever have any) to incorporate her modulations,
As deeply as rocking, rocking to her breathing,
When they are so young and new, that breathing
And being alive are indistinguishable.

*You're only as Jung as you feel.*
A birthday card accuses the generic me
Of over-analysis of footprints.
I sing to the ocean. April pants.
The sun sinks. Woodstock licks my toes.
My thumb toes make me laugh, which is
Why I enameled them blue.

VI

And what about the days the sap runs slow?
It still hits eighty at noon.
Women change to white sling-backs at work.
Their men drive home, bare-armed, to squirt
Lighter fluid onto the grill, but I can
Barely see the corners of the living room,
Because the angle of the light has
Changed, like sleep coming on, and the
Air on the balcony has a
Yellow snap to it.

VII

Dead grasshopper—
Wings like two secrets
Folded beneath two whispers,
One antenna clasped between forelegs
Like a lullaby half-bowed—
Were you the persistent suitor under

The window of my gray-green,
Summer sleep—shell of summer,
Perfect last breath—
Condensed on the balcony
In the first cold snap?

VIII

And what of the soul?
A gray-green shadow on the wings of the dove?
A flare in the nostrils of the Angel of Death?
The infinite will to live; our painful difference.
Dad doing mouth-to-mouth on the cat
Because of the look in Mom's eyes when
The fleas abandoned it—fur warm, body the
Temperature of stone, stone retaining itself.
Living creatures disembodied.
Will to live is not the same as fear to die.
Will to live is the soul reveling in its sensateness,
Not wanting to be alone.

IX

And what of reaffirmation?
Getting out of bed another morning
Of wet leaves mingled with car exhaust
And recycled rain and hitting the road,
Again, in a random cape of buttons,
Scattered like pre-migration heebee-jeebees.
Rally round the Messiah,
Panhandle the Promise.
We are prophets, primping, beggars on the line,
Bounced from neighborhoods we
Uniformed ourselves.

Pre-judged,
Living in memory—
The next generation,

Phenotypically ours,
Masters our prejudices
With our earlobes—brain
Geology pre-empting words.
Ancestor signs: the song of
Many dreams, the coat of
Many buttons.

At five I wanted to be buried, fully
Clothed, with an acorn in my palm.
By twenty, I understood transformation
To be the discarding of uniforms. (Let
The naked courtyard catch me.) By now,
I suspect what's left of my DNA will
Opacify the Atlantic with filaments of
Toilet paper, retroviruses, polyesters—
Human Overwaste—that yet can
Jewel unfiltered sunlight for the
Raiments of the sea.

And what of last breath?
A gouged, elaborate button
From the bottom of the tin
A mockery of posture
Last arctic button breath
If I am lucky, a hand holds mine.
We are old enough to know God
And what it's not, to package Fear,
Disobey Time, answer curtain calls
Manipulate Redemption. God is the
Universe, sifting through the button
Box, selecting smooth minds,
Reducing symmetries,
Passing on breath,
Breath acquiring meaning,
Meaning learned and relearned,
Knowledge the means to survive
And destroy, Mortal Arrogance.

When I was eight I held the cord
To the Venetian blinds in the window
To my brother's room, (the girls' room having
Been the upstairs porch). My sister asked
Questions endlessly: Nature, God.
I answered in handfuls, convinced that
What transpires matters. She admitted, later,
A voice, any voice, would banish
"Wild animals" to beyond the door she opened,
Nightly, "just a crack," keeping me up,
Until I heard her innocent ivory button
Breaths and shut the door.

I held the cord to say
Goodnight to the world,
Because the cord touched the
Blinds that touched the window
That touched my brother in his bed.
The bed touched the world that touched
All things breathing and not breathing
That touched my mother's shoulder
And the night in which we rocked and sang.

## Doc pushes steroids/Family speaks in tongues

and, between the uncharted continents of us, the septic,
late-amniocentesis ocean of herself, Sillette pulls through.
Mind you,

she has been on 'jet fuel' for days—shock lungs, shock liver,
shock kidneys, shock adrenals—fibrin and platelets caulking
and uncaulking

in the everywhere leaking retroperitoneum, uterus a maelstrom
of birth and afterbirth. The infant delivers stillborn, an empty
skiff in

the schooner of her arms, hers and Bill's, before she heads,
hell-bent, for the cliffs. We load her with antibiotics, sedatives,
saline,

blood products, catechols. Three young sons enlist us to sign
get-well cards at the nurses' station. Doc pushes steroids.
Family beacons,

coasts, coaxes, keels in tongues. What syllables in its swell?
How the squalling moves and frightens, comforts and sustains
us. It

quiets when we hoist the sign. Another sick ship coming in.
It sighs in tidal waves, typhoons, in ripples, ruffles, and in
pools. Speaking

tongues. Not stopping, not even when Sillette does. We
dialyze. It is not clear why she does not bleed in rivers to
her death. Then,

six weeks later, she walks out. Wants to try again. Trach is
closing, memory, an undercurrent, not remembering. We are
holds unto

ourselves. There must be body—in and of and around
water, weather, harbor, murmurings not hers or ours—
that rocks, keeps, sings and sails her.

# Sestina: Unwrapped

And I remembered a mummy in the Vatican Museum in Rome: in her sarcophagus shaped
and painted like herself, an Egyptian girl 2000 years old lay unwrapped to the waist, and
with hands and feet bare—her nails, hair, lips and eyelids frangible as tobacco leaf, but intact.
Still exquisite, merely dried and darkened was her youth.      —May Swenson

It is the distance traveled,

Her stenciled youth,

lashes, and her skin's

Translucent beauty,

merely transilluminated

From an unmarked Ecuadoran town

to this

darkened sarcophagus-city

Where hope is dried long before

a cure is conjured

And      exquisite tears

lie painted on the bed

—Unearth her still.

The surgeons who found

The mass still cured all masses

                                        with excision.
Because of youth

                                and its alchemies,

She survived the scalpel's

                exquisite inability to differentiate

Bowel from tumor;

                        merely took what they could see and

saw too much.

                She dried slowly, salvaged

                                        from the rising

river bank as NYC darkened

In her room and wrapped her—

                darkened

                        cylinder,

                        hands, feet, ink-dark

Eyes (unopened still)—

                        in city swaddling

(Pediatric gown, traffic wads,

dried river dregs,

Pigeon-spackled drapes of dyers' woad),

Youth as impotent as Age

To summon merely what is just or just expected:

this exquisite

Child,    shipped to us

wrapped as achingly in hope as

An exquisite child Egyptian,

age—2000 years,

Painted,   darkened, inevitable, illegible,

museum piece,

Leaf merely drying.

She will outlive the Vatican.

Still, she is neither god nor gilded, but

Man,    girl,

Child, Eternal Youth,

Hope recorded, History begun, reed

Erased by tears dried


On the open face

Of an entire village that dried

the mother's face, peso by peso,

(from Exquisite, Teacher, Tradesman, Mayor,

Priest)

To pay the fee for hospital,

post mother, aunt, child

On their unappointed journey,

so Youth, this skinny crucifer could

Triumph over cancer, darkened berths,

schooled surgeons,

calyx, kiln,

Cathedral.    Still,

merely,

To have arrived was

so miraculous,

Mother and aunt merely

relinquished her

to the auriferous–

Mecca,

tectonics,

hope;

dried the plated brows,

Intoned prayers to dark, still pearls, the

inlaid filamentous lids;

And almost believed

exquisite Illumination

culls life from art

In hospitals.

The child darkened

(as we knew she would),

Vessel,

kylix El Diablo would craft,

Whose craft is

Death-in-life and -youth.




Still

In hospital wrapping,

Exquisite

in porcelain repose,

"merely

dried and

darkened

was her

youth."

## progress note

.prostaglandin vaginal suppository-induced abortion .twenty-one
weeks     .nurse has left the fetus on the office chair to take polaroids
*.this pregnancy is killing my patient*     *.she is waiting for her only brother
to arrive from Eritrea .she does not know he is murdered     .her husband forbids
that she be told* .I do not know she's gone ahead with an abortion and
have come to talk it over


## Lullabye Little Fish
(for Fetus S. and his mother and me)


Little fish
      Little fish

            Little shoe
              Little cell

Lullabye
      Lullalull

            Without scale
              Without gill

Without suck
      Without shore

            Little sail
              Little sir

Little cone
      Little conch

            *In the brim*
          *of my chair*

            —

Mr. Bluer-than-blue

Born-not-to-be-born

Little fist
    Little fist

        Lullabye
           Lullalost

Little slip
    Little shoal

        Little pause
           Little shelf

*She has not*
    *yet been told*

        Blue passport
           Blue pool

*Her brother's*
    *been shot*

        Lullalisp
           Lulla'no'

Little fist
    Little furl

        Little sill
           Little shock

Blue hairline
    Blue prow

        Little varicose curl

Little boat
Little bed

Little boy
Lullabye

*His name is*
*Your name*

*Your name is*
*His prayer*

—

*(A child, mine, would*
*be five if...*

*He pulled out*
*He lied )*

There must be a Kaddish

*Wet Parkway*
*Blue car*

I'd stroked her
we'd talked

*Blue portal*
*Blue lips*

*(Not AIDS, can't*
*get angry*

*Born-not-to-be-born)*

Near death on
    the Parkway

        *Blue maybe*
           *Blue veil*

Young, crying
    redhead

        Asleep at
           the wheel

NPR,
    coffee

        Vehicular
           steel

Exit: Cathedral

        *Blue archway*
           *Blue curves*

Alley, deck,
    kitchen,

        *Blue hallway,*
           *Blue heads*

*No chair*
    *seems empty*

        *Blue hollow*
           *Blue cowl*

—

Lullabye
    Little fish

           Little fist
            Little boy
Little lie
    Lulla'no'

        Lulla'if'
          Lullalull

Lullabye
    Little moon

        *Little man*
    *Lullabye*

—

## addendum

.*some women are closer to having an accident than a baby*    .Mr. S. has called today .sending wife to Canada to visit sister  .Mrs. S. cannot stop crying .*no chair seems empty*   ."sorry," he says, "telling it—*doctor* forbid me" .*I believe* .*if she had known she would have*  .*kept and named*

## The Gesture

...As water given sugar sweetens, given salt grows salty,
we become our choices.
Each *yes*, each *no* continues,
this one a ladder, that one an anvil or cup.

...How can I enter this question the clay has asked?
—Jane Hirshfield 'Rebus' *Given Sugar, Given Salt*


*As water given sugar sweetens, given salt grows salty /*
*we become our choices.* Would that that were so.
Clean slice of page,

of course she did not know. Here she lies in sinking and
in falling, the color of the M.E.'s table,
as full of salt

and sugar—saline, dextrose—as any clay can turn away from.
Clay doesn't ask. It doesn't have to. It is its own
signature and masque.

If I could heal a little better, I would dry her to a small white
heap—there is dignity in dryness, a word of comfort,
thirty pills, acetominophen—

and put her in your palm, imperfect powder, fallen ladder
from the days she'd gotten through, anvil of the
here-and-now... empty cup.

## Self-Portrait

Destination, in the land of never enough,
       is the cornice of all I can give/all that I know,
          given over to deep blue sky.


The confirmation of poet is doctor;
       the consummation of doctor is poet.
          I have a black, silk-velvet gown.


In the composite, stranger/oh most intimate
       incarnates the lens, eyes promontory, body oblique.
          Her lover is a dried red rose.


At her feet, finch eggs in a blue ceramic cone.
       The injured pigeon, now set free, nestles at her hem.
          She is barefoot, primed to fly/to fall.


End print, half-kneeling, deep set in dark, clavicles
       encrypt snow-angel wings/the stethoscope's repose and
          constellate the white line of her throat.

# NOTES ON THE POEMS

**Night Shift**
This poem takes place in the Emergency Room (E.R.) at Bellevue Hospital in New York City. It was the beginning of the AIDS epidemic and before antiretroviral drugs. It was just after New York City closed 1,500 beds and began flying in nurses from the Philippines and elsewhere to ease the nursing shortage that accompanied the bed shortage. The poem is structured as a series of encounters with patients, woven together by the Yom Kippur liturgy, with the Hebrew in transliteration and then translation.

Medical terms by section: II—*Narcan*, brand name for nalaxone, an opiate antagonist that immediately reverses opiate overdose; a patient can be blue and not breathing on admission and wild and awake in an instant after receiving the medication. III—*Inderal*, brand name for propanolol, a cardiac medication that slows heart rate; also used in extreme anxiety; can be fatal with overdose. *Halcion*—sedative used for sleep and anxiety; can be fatal with overdose. V—*trach*, short for tracheostomy, a hole in the trachea (windpipe) for patients who are on respirators or cannot clear their own secretions. VI—*toxic prognosis*, a malapropism for an infectious disease of the brain, toxoplasmosis, seen in AIDS patients. VIII—*hemorrhagic cystitis*, bleeding from the bladder; bladder cancer has been related to certain red dyes in hair color; the latter are no longer used in coloring products. XI—*vaginal discharge*, fluid or pus from the vagina.

**The Angio**
*Angio*—short for angiogram, an x-ray study during which a dye is injected into the arteries supplying the heart; the dye shows up on a screen and blockages can be diagnosed.

**Heroes**
*Kwell*—brand name of a shampoo that kills lice. *Nodes*—lymph glands. *Latex*—plastic from which surgical gloves are made.

**Grandbaby Doe**
*'Dotted Q'*—term hospital personnel use when a fly lands on the tongue of a person sleeping with the tongue hanging out of the mouth; indicates a certain lack of awareness of surroundings, neurologic impairment, or heavy sedation.

**The Train Wreck**
A post-cardiac surgery patient in the ICU had a surgical complication. The surgeons opened his chest in the bed and covered the heart with a laparotomy cloth (drape). While I was watching him until he could be taken back to the operating room for definitive treatment, I overheard a young nurse with a thick Irish brogue tell her comrades the story of a woman who had not gotten up to give a nun a seat on the train. The train was involved in a wreck, and as the woman got out of the train, she stepped on something that she realized was the severed head of the nun. The story became inextricable in my memory from trying to stabilize the critically ill gentleman in the ICU bed. A complicated patient or one with multiple, severe injuries is frequently referred to, in ICU jargon, as a 'train wreck'.

**Belladonna**
*Belladonna*—poisonous plant also called Deadly Nightshade; has medical uses and is used on the street; it was also used in ancient Rome to dilate pupils, which was thought to enhance the beauty of a woman; it is used today to dilate pupils for eye examination; one price of beauty for Roman women appears to have been

blurry vision. *Mydriasis*—dilated pupils; *Accommodation*—the reaction of the pupil of one eye to the amount of light hitting the pupil of the other. *Mad as a hatter, hot as a hare, red as a beet, dry as a bone*—pneumonic used in the ER to remember the signs of belladonna alkaloid overdose.

### I Want You In A Suit

*CPR*—cardiopulmonary resuscitation. *Prosthesis*—mechanical devise, e.g. artificial leg, mechanical valve, hip replacement, penile implant.

### Northeast Coast Corridor

The title refers to the Amtrak train route from Washington, DC to New York City and other cities along the northeastern seaboard.

Medical terms by section: II—*C-4 quad,* quadriplegic at the fourth cervical vertebra, paralyzed and without sensation from the neck down; since patients require mechanical ventilation and have a tube in the trachea they communicate by smacking their lips or blinking their eyes. *Rotobed,* special bed to stabilize the spine; the arms are held out in the form of a 'T' so the body is in the shape of a cross. III—*TRENTON MAKES THE WORLD TAKES,* motto on a bridge trellis visible from the tracks as you approach the train station at Trenton, NJ. VI—University Hospital, at the time of the incident with the editor, had just been renamed Tisch-NYU in honor of a significant donor; Bellevue was the referral ER for prisoners from Riker's Island.

### Power not Peace

*Shit flows downhill*—a frequent answer to the question "Why do I have to do this?" when you are an intern. *Arrests*—suffers cardiopulmonary arrest. *Code*—cardiopulmonary resuscitation procedures.

### In Presumed Innocence

*Crepitance*—sensation to the touch like Rice Krispies due to air under the skin; seen with trauma. *Female circumcision*—also known as female genital mutilation (FMG), various forms of mutilating the external genitalia, including clitoral excision in extreme cases, to insure the virginity of a young woman; seen not infrequently in woman seeking asylum in this country.

### Blood Holies

In the surgical intensive care unit (ICU) we took care of a young woman whose small car had collided with a truck on the Beltway outside Washington. DC. She sustained extensive pelvic injury. This type of injury bleeds massively. The surgeons took her back to the operating room (OR) many times in an effort to save her. In between OR trips we poured fluids and blood products into her, hundreds of units. She died quietly before morning.

When I got home, I read the first accounts in *The Washington Post* of the genocide in the former Yugoslavia. One of the reports was from Visegrad, a small town overlooking the Drina River. The article mentions that the bridge from which people were being thrown had been written about by Ivo Andric, a Serb writer who received the Nobel Prize for Literature (1961). Andric's contribution to the history of the Balkans is substantial. He had been placed under house arrest for three years, during World War I, with a view of that very bridge. The name of his most well-known work is *Bridge Over the Drina*. He uses the bridge as a thread with which to follow the complex and heart-rending history of his conflicted homeland, the tinderbox for two world wars.

As I read about the history of the bridge and the Balkans, I wondered about the nature of conquest. Why did it so often involve humiliation and disfigurement, very often of a sexual nature? That is, what is the re-lationship of violence to arousal? I use arousal, here, in its physiological sense. A fellow poet and psychiatrist directed me to the work of Robert Stoller, MD. The latter wrote careful, detailed studies, describing and defining, among other researches, the origin of perversity, which he defines as the 'erotic form of hatred'. On the scale of genocide, it becomes almost impossible for most of us to accept or acknowledge that such behavior is going on. In fact, mass killing instigates 'silence'. The newspaper reporter is careful to say that the man initially reporting the atrocities had lost his journal, and, therefore, what he described could not be verified.

Medical terms by section: I—*Critical time,* the one hour after injury during which start of treatment has the best outcome, especially for shock states. *Hemovac,* brand name of a tube that is used to drain a wound or body cavity and that works by suction. *Proteinaceous*—contains protein and congeals; blood has this property. IV—*Onanism,* masterbation. V—*'vila' of the waters,* water spirit.

### 551,880,000 Breaths

Medical terms by section: I—*lungers,* patients with trouble breathing, usually due to chronic pulmonary disease. *Nasal prongs*—tubing that delivers oxygen through the nostrils. III—*Sternum,* breast bone. *Phalanx,* finger bone. *Pectoral flap,* flap of chest wall muscle used to cover the heart when part of the ribcage has been removed. IV—*C-section,* cesarean section. *Ventricles,* central spaces in the brain. *Definitions of death*—physiologically, a cessation of cardiac and pulmonary function, or irreversible injury to vital structures in the brain required to maintain cardiopulmonary function; medico-legally, when a patient meets criteria for clinical brain death; a diagnosis of clinical brain death allows withdrawal of equipment that sustains cardio-pulmonary function, but cannot reverse brain death which is terminal.

### Doc pushes steroids/Family speaks in tongues

Medical terms: *Septic*—showing signs of shock, due to infection. *Amniocentesis*—sampling of amniotic fluid while a fetus is *in utero*. On *'jet fuel'*—requiring potent medications to maintain vital signs, like blood pressure. *Retroperi-toneum*—cavity behind the perineum, where the uterus and other organs are located. *Catechols*—catecholamines; vasoactive substances used to increase blood pressure in shock. *Dialyze*—perform dialysis; filter the blood when the kidneys fail; in this case it is done through veins because the patient is so unstable; it has a high likelihood of exacerbating bleeding tendencies which are elevated in sepsis. *Trach*—tracheostomy (see **'Night Shift'**,V)

### Sestina: Unwrapped

When I was a Fellow in Critical Care we took care of a six-year-old girl from Central America. She had a bowel lymphoma on which local surgeons had operated. For further treatment, she was accepted to our tertiary cancer hospital, a 'mecca' for this type of care in New York City. Her entire village gathered every peso they had from everyone in her village so that her mother and aunt could bring her here. The hospital, at that time, required an admission fee equal to double that of the expected stay for non-citizens. The predicted fee was $25,000. Tragically, when the girl was evaluated, it became clear the amount of bowel already removed made survival impossible. When she died she was so translucent and beautiful. Her family was inconsolable.

Medical terms: *Transillumination*—shine fiberoptic light through a hollow organ like the bowel to locate the tip of an instrument, e.g. an endoscope. *Drapes*—sterile cloth or paper used to keep an operative site clean; usually royal blue or green in color. *Dyers' woad*—dark blue color derived from the leaves of crucifers; the plant from which it is derived, *Isatis tinctoria*; blue dye obtained from the woad plant and used in ancient times as a body paint. *Crucifer*—evergreen plant with a flower that has four petals in the shape of a cross. *Calyx*—group of sepals, usually green, that enclose and protect a flower bud. *Kylix*—shallow two-handled cup, often with a footed stem.

**Lullabye Little Fish**

Medical terms: *Progress note*—written medical record of all hospital events; usually written daily. *Addendum*—additions or follow-up to the daily progress note. *Prostaglandin vaginal suppository*—medication used to dilate the cervix during induced labor.

**The Gesture**

The young woman in this poem was in shock and fulminant liver failure after overdosing on Tylenol. She was 19 years old. While waiting the requisite 24 hours to determine clinical brain death due to irreversible swelling, we reversed profound shock and had her accepted for transfer to an institution that could do a liver transplant. She had twenty-three family members holding vigil in the small waiting room and enduring the wait. They showed me the picture on her driver's license, so I could see what she looked like before being hospitalized and becoming barely recognizable. After determining that there was no blood flow to her brain, the respirator was switched off. Her parents held her hand, whispering their goodbyes.

Medical terms: *M.E.*—medical examiner. *Acetominophen*—generic name for Tylenol; frequently used in suicide gestures, but can be fatal if a certain amount is ingested.

# ACKNOWLEDGMENTS

Grateful acknowledgement is made to the publications in which the following poems origi-
nally appeared: 'The Angio', 'Power Not Peace', 'Another Drive-by', and 'Self-Portrait', in the
*Paris Review*; 'All that Separates' and 'Counting Backwards' from '551,880,000 Breaths' in the
*Journal of the American Medical Association (JAMA)*.

Mom, Dad, Mutti, Daniel B., Judy, Joyce, Shira, Gavi, Grandpa Max, Grandpa Friedel and the
whole menagerie, no words are deep enough.

An abundance of understanding, kindness and substantial 'technical' assistance has come my
way, both over time and at crucial moments. To everyone who has understood my medical and
artistic drives and dreams, thank you, from my heart to yours. So many people from so many
spheres of my life come to mind that it is not possible to name you all. I will, nevertheless,
take a moment to acknowledge some of the people who either contributed directly to making
*Night Shift* a reality, or who validated my simultaneous existence in the worlds of medicine
and poetry.

Special thanks to Patti Capaldi, for designing the book, letter by letter; to Kevin Walzer and
Lori Jareo of Turning Point for accepting the manuscript; and to David Fenza (my Mac maven)
for everything and then some. For various infusions of humanity, attention, beauty, love and
hope, thanks to Jaqueline Austin, Eva Avi-Yonah, Linda Ayers-Frederick, Maya Boyko, Char-
lotte Breedlove, Melissa Crown, Lewis Goldfrank, Beatrice Greenberg, Anthony Grieco, Jan
Grossman, Michael Hauptschein, Richard Howard, Alex Jamison, Patricia Spears Jones, Harley
Kaufman, Galway Kinnell, Lee Kravitz, April Land, Vicki Marani, Helen Meyers, Trudy-Gilah
Morse, Misako Nakama, Howard Norman, Sharon Olds, Molly Peacock, Robert Pinsky, Grace
Rozycki, Len Rubinstein, Gerda Schulman, John Schumacher, George Liston Seay, Penelope
Shambly-Schott, Jane Shore, Pauline Smolin, John Stern, Tree Swenson, Max Ticktin, Elisabeth
Waltuch, and James Woolery. Thanks to Princess Victoria Peccoo and Richard Caleskie for
enabling my parents to be home together in a touch-and-go year.

I would also like to recognize a few of the communities that shaped my sensibilities or offered
protected space and time: the Squaw Valley Community of Writers, the Virginia Center for
Creative Arts, the Helene Wurlitzer Foundation, and the MacDowell Colony; Yale University;
NYU School of Medicine and Surgical Critical Care Associates; Physicians for Human Rights;
the Center for Bioethics, Washington Hospital Center; Unity Woods Yoga Center; Feathered
Pipe Ranch; Fabrangan; Hadassah and Gayla's kitchen.

And last, but not least, for loyalty and joyousness, I am thankful for the Finches, Buster, Elliot,
Twinkie, Simmie, Fox, Woodstock, Willie and Zena.

## ABOUT THE AUTHOR

For 20 years Serena J. Fox has practiced intensive care medicine in Washington, DC. She is also a consultant in bedside medical ethics and a human rights advocate. Her career was launched in the emergency room of Bellevue Hospital in New York City. She believes deeply that poetry and the humanities have essential roles in the teaching of medicine and care-giving. Her poems have appeared in the *Paris Review*, the *Journal of the American Medical Association* and the *Western Humanities Review.*

*Photo of the author in 1989*